HIGHBRI
IN ITS HEYDAY

HOME OF THE SOMERSET AND
DORSET RAILWAY

by
Colin G. Maggs

THE OAKWOOD PRESS

©Oakwood Press and C. G. Maggs 1986
ISBN 0 85361 324 9
Printed by Bocardo Press, Cowley, Oxford

First published 1973

Frontispiece: Highbridge Great Western Station, showing the Somerset and Dorset Railway Branch to Burnham-on-Sea crossing the GWR main line from left to right.

Nelson Collection

Published by
The Oakwood Press
P. O. Box 122
Headington, Oxford

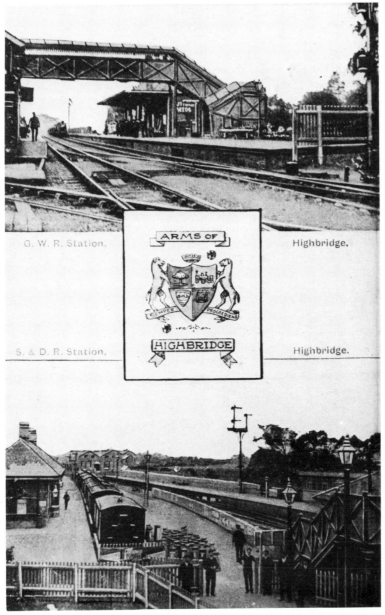

G. W. R. Station,   Highbridge.

ARMS OF

HIGHBRIDGE

S. & D. R. Station,   Highbridge.

Plate 1: An early composite photograph incorporating the Highbridge
Town Coat of Arms, and showing the GWR Station (looking west) with the
S&D line crossing in the foreground and, in the lower section, the S&D
Station at Highbridge with the Works in the background. The footbridge in
the bottom left hand corner of the photograph, joins the footbridge of the
upper (GWR) photograph.

Author's Collection

FOREWORD

This book makes no attempt to compete with the histories of the Somerset & Dorset Railway already published, but is intended to supplement them, showing perspectives of Somerset & Dorset equipment and practice not noted elsewhere.

Few railways have had recorded such fascinating details of methods of carriage and wagon building, locomotive water supply and so on, as is to be found in this book, yet these items were very essential to the running of a line.

The author has gathered much information during the many pleasurable hours he has spent with 'S.F.R.', whose unique recollections of his period of service at Highbridge Works and Bath Locomotive Depot from 1910 until retirement in 1960, form the bulk of this book. S.F.R.'s post at Highbridge brought him into unusually close contact with all departments of the locomotive, carriage and wagon works. He kept detailed notebooks from the 1930s to 1960, while earlier information he culled partly from records and partly from memory. In cases where accuracy may be in doubt, the text makes this clear.

The author thanks the photographers whose names are noted in the captions. The remainder are official SDJR photographs, which British Rail have courteously allowed to be reproduced. Thanks are also due to BR for permission to reproduce the locomotive depot plans.

Bath, 1972   Colin G. Maggs

FOREWORD TO SECOND EDITION

This new edition has incorporated a few minor additions and corrections to the original work, and has allowed a greatly expanded photographic coverage to give a more comprehensive pictorial survey of this popular railway.

Bath, 1986   Colin G. Maggs

Contents

Plate 2: A very early view of Highbridge Station looking in the down direction showing the layout of the station, signal gantry, ornate lights, the Works in the background and above all the period costumes of the passengers.

Author's Collection

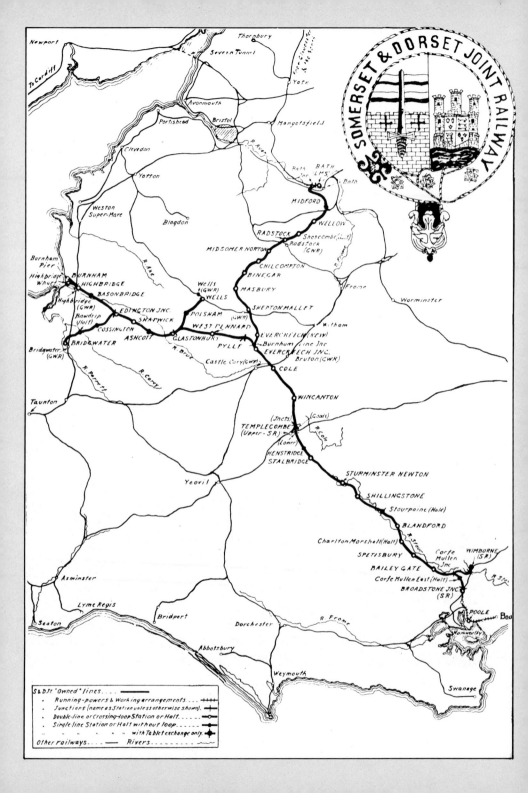

Chapter One

Highbridge Works

Highbridge Works was opened by the Somerset and Dorset Railway in 1862. The buildings were added rather haphazardly and the factory was re-organised by the locomotive superintendent, Alfred Whitaker, in the 1890s, when a stores and paint shop were built. Workshop doors were painted cream and light brown; window frames were also this latter colour, while the interior walls were white-washed.

The locomotive works are seen in a transitional period *Plate 3 (taken circa 1895)* with the new boiler-shop, coppersmiths' shop and foundry building almost ready for occupation. The buildings, *left to right* are: the messroom (the small lean-to at its side housed a solid-tyred wheel stretcher, the only official first aid equipment at the works); the sheer legs with a tender suspended beneath it; the old wooden boiler-shop with boilersmiths' forge chimney at the right. Behind these a block contained the superintendent's drawing and general offices, brass and iron foundry, springsmiths' forges and case hardening furnace, blacksmiths' forge, steam hammer and the machine shop with lathes, drilling, shaping, lapping, grinding and screw cutting machines. The darker structure with end-to-end roof lights was the erecting shop. The paler building, not completed, had not yet been brought into full use as boilershop, coppersmiths' shop and foundry. The tyre hearth chimney had

Plate 3: A fine view of the Works at Highbridge photographed c. 1895.
Author's Collection

not been built. Dominating the rear is the chimney of the locomotive department stationary engine boiler — the Works' power house.

The spot where the unidentified coach is standing was frequently the resting place for coaches awaiting repairs, or standing ready to go into traffic after repairs and painting were completed. Overhead was the steam pipeline from the stationary boiler to the erecting shop gantry engine and from it, to the saw-mill engine. A boiler-house was eventually built and the pipeline removed, only to be temporarily reinstated when boiler repairs were undertaken. A large brick chimney replaced the tiny exhaust steam pipe which shows over the top of the sawmill gantry of wooden posts. The area under the gantry was fairly well stocked with rough logs.

The dark building on the right was the gas fitter's workshop. He was also the plumber and, in later years, the electrician too and was responsible for fitting gas burners to replace the oil lamps, and electric light to replace the gas burners. The wheels were awaiting electric bonding to complete track circuits. Behind the shed was the loco foreman's cottage.

Plate 4 shows Highbridge Works locomotive erecting & fitting shop before 1895. The photograph was taken at a very busy period; six engines are in

Plate 4: A pre 1895 view of the locomotive erecting and fitting shop at Highbridge Works with at least six locomotives being worked upon. The wheel turning lathe can be seen in the distant corner.

Author's Collection

various stages of repair and it is reasonable to suppose that two or even three more were under the gantry from which the picture was taken. Sunlight is shining through the windows on the south side, which dates the picture before 1895, as there could be no sunshine after the building of the new bay to house the foundry, coppersmiths' and boiler shop along the whole of that side.

Attached to the wall in the left hand corner was the workshop gantry steam engine, *(Plate 5)* and overhead along the left wall can be seen the rope drive to power the gantry. The machinery in the right hand corner was a hydraulic press for putting tyres on wheels and wheels on axles; a large engine wheel lathe; carriage wheel lathe and two wagon wheel lathes. Shafting for powering these was attached to the wall under the overhead gantry rail, the original drive being from the locomotive stationary engine transferred by belt from shafting the other side of the wall.

When this picture was taken there was just the fire pump house and the 'Bosh' outside the building behind the windows. The 'Bosh' was a steam heated water tank with a heavy perforated false bottom about 2 ft from the surface and about 12 ft by 6 ft with a safety rail guarding it. Into this tank was lowered all kinds of dirty, greasy materials to be boiled clean in a soda solution before inspection and repairs were carried out.

To transfer a locomotive from one road to another inside the shop, the overhead gantry crane was used in conjunction with an inclined runway. The front of the engine was lifted on to the runway by gantry, then the rear slewed over. This economical traverser was invented by Alfred Whitaker. On the left-hand road is 4-4-0 locomotive No. 15 with an 0-6-0, No. 46, beyond. At the far end of the shop is seen one of the Radstock shunting engines.

There was no road access to the Works, just an ash path known as the 'black path', until American troops built one during World War II. In S&D times, any cart built there had to be taken away by rail.

From 1879 to 1898 the numbers on the staff at Highbridge varied between 344 and 485 men.

The work-force was fairly stable. The period of service of staff employed by the S&D Locomotive, Carriage & Wagon Departments between 20th October, 1861 and 28th December, 1899 was as follows:

Completed less than 1 year	494 staff
Completed 1 - 10 years	762
Completed 11 - 20 years	139
Completed 21 - 30 years	93
Completed 31 - 40 years	113
Completed 41 - 50 years	182
Completed 51 and upwards	25
	1808

Plate 5: The highly polished gantry engine in the erecting shop. Note the ropes on the right; these were made from hemp.

Author's Collection

Very soon after the retirement of Alfred Whitaker in July 1911, the arrival of M. F. Ryan saw the commencement of the decline of the Works. Almost immediately new wagon building was phased out. Wagon builders were transferred to the Midland Railway's shops at Bristol, LSWR shops at Eastleigh, or they simply left as they became redundant. The same applied to carriage builders when construction of new bogie coaches ended. However, conversions from gas to electric lighting of vehicles was carried on long after new coach building ended. Finally the oil gas plant at Higbridge Loco closed.

Two or more S&D bogie coaches were permanently on loan to the MR and ran between Bristol and Bradford to balance Midland vehicles which worked trains between Bath and Bournemouth West over S&D lines. Running repairs to this S&D stock were carried out at Bristol by men from Highbridge Works — vacuum brake examiner, gas fitter cum electrician, and mates. The men always travelled by S&D and MR via Evercreech Junction and Bath, a distance of 64 miles each way, as no free passes were available over the direct GWR line, (27 miles), and the privilege ticket fare of 1s. 1½d. was considered an unnecessary expense. For heavy repairs, exchange of coaches was made via Bath. These workmen from Highbridge were issued with special forms which required the station master's signature stating time of arrival, whether meal time was worked and time of departure for home.

The buff coloured shed housing the wheeled ambulance stretcher at the end of the messroom was removed so that the War Memorial could be put in its place where all entering the Loco Works could see it. Designed by apprentice fitter Harold John Kitch, it was cast in the foundry at Highbridge by patternmaker J. T. Ardish, the keeper of the Carriage and Wagon Department stores, E. G. N. Baker carving the lettering and decoration. On 8th March, 1922 the Memorial was unveiled by Sir Allan Garrett Anderson KBE and dedicated by the Lord Bishop of Bath and Wells.

The following notice appeared on 10th November, 1920:

It is the wish of His Majesty the King that, as on the last anniversary of Armistice Day, there should be a complete suspension of normal business and locomotion for two minutes, at 11.00 a.m. on 11th November, 1920 as far as this may be practicable, together with cession of sound from engines etc; as a simple Silent Service in reverent remembrance of the Glorious Dead.

In order that all men may be afforded this opportunity:-

(a) All work will cease in Offices, and Loco Sheds etc, at 11.00 o'clock for two minutes, the shop engines at Highbridge Workshops and Bath repair depot being stopped for 5 minutes.

(b) Trains ready to leave a Station or Signal at 11.00 a.m. to be detained for 2 minutes.

(c) Trains in motion at 11.00 a.m. to be brought to a stand as near as possible to that time, but in complying therewith enginemen must avoid bringing the train to rest on a steep rising gradient, in a tunnel, or on a high Viaduct or Bridge.

R. C. Archbutt
Res. Loco. Supt.

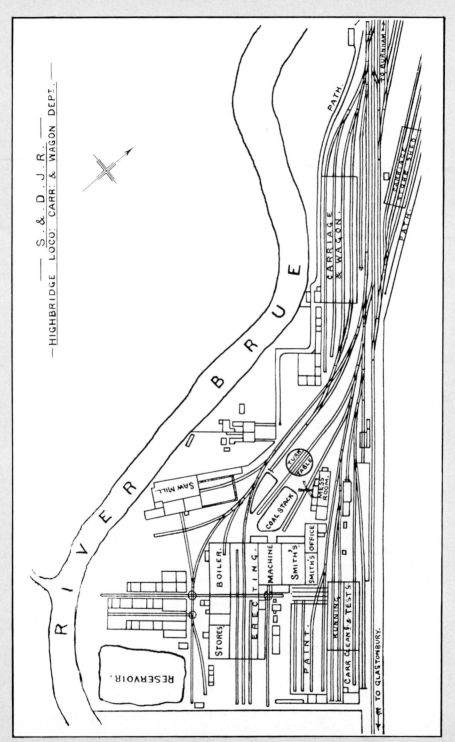

Plan of Highbridge Locomotive, Carriage and Wagon Works in the 1920s.

Plate 6: The commencement of a new wagon! This photograph taken in the carriage and wagon shop shows well the variety of goods stock with at least eighteen different wagons on view.

W. Bruce Champion Collection

Plate 7: The carriage makers' shop is captured in this posed photograph and the carriage detail is worthy of note. Eleven young apprentices appear in this view.

W. Bruce Champion Collection

Plate 8: Even more employees are seen in this view of the paint shop. Note the heating pipes on the floor to keep the shop at a fairly constant temperature to dry the paint.

W. Bruce Champion Collection

Plate 9: One of the 'noisy' shops at Highbridge was the boiler shop, seen here with two boilers in for repair.

W. Bruce Champion Collection

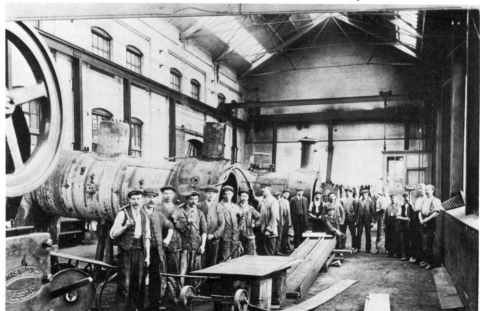

Plate 10: No. 28 seen here in the Works running shop with a tender cab and further engines in evidence.

W. Bruce Champion Collection

Plate 11: Attached to the erecting shop (as a lean-to) was the fitters' shop. Here the fitters 'hand' cleaned, filed and fitted bearings, links, coupling rods etc, all of which can be seen in the photograph.

W. Bruce Champion Collection

Plate 12: A very important part of the Works was the General Stores. Here the staff pose for their photograph. Note the axle boxes between the tracks.

W. Bruce Champion Collection

Plate 13: The making of springs was a very important job in a Railway Works and here at Highbridge, was no exception. The photograph certainly shows the 'strong arm' brigade.

W. Bruce Champion Collection

Plate 14: The coppersmiths' shop where the big-end liners were prepared for re-metalling.

W. Bruce Champion Collection

Plate 15: Another important shop, sometimes overlooked in the glamour of railway work was the general blacksmiths' shop, capable of making, mending and fixing anything!

W. Bruce Champion Collection

Plate 16: The War Memorial in Highbridge Works on November 11th, sometime in the 1920s.

Author's Collection

Plate 17: A view of Highbridge S&D 'A' signal box, with an 0-4-4T coming off the Burnham-on-Sea Branch just about to cross the GWR main line at right angles. The roof of the GWR signal box can be seen middle-left with the road bridge seen under the footbridge.

Author's Collection

Plate 18: A view of Highbridge crossing in the 1920s looking from the front of the engine in the last plate. This shows the GWR signal box and its unique shape plus the GWR Station. The S&D Station can be seen to the left of the signal box. The GWR main line runs from Bristol (left) to Exeter (right).

Bath Railway Society

From Edington Junction to Highbridge 'C' box sited by the large stone shed opposite the carriage & wagon erecting shop, the line was worked by electric tablet; from 'C' box through the passenger station to the GWR Highbridge Crossing box was standard double line working. Across the GWR's Bristol to Exeter main line from Highbridge Crossing to 'B' box, and 'B' to 'A' was worked by staff and ticket regulations without staff or ticket, and the line from 'A' box to Burnham (the Branch) was worked by staff and ticket.

The original 'A' signal box was sited at the west end of No. 4, one of the bay platforms and although closed in 1914 remained as a guards' mess room. 'B' box, west of the GWR line also controlled a road level crossing, while 'C' signal box (controlling a crossing over the A38) was at the east end of the Highbridge Wharf complex.*

The Great Western Highbridge Crossing signal box built in 1913 was a 'one-off' pattern to fit in the cramped position between the S&DJR and GWR lines, one end having to be wedge-shaped *(see Plate 18)*.

---

*Before nationalisation the signal boxes were Highbridge Loco, 'A' (closed 1914), 'B' and 'C'. After nationalisation 'Loco' became 'C' and 'C' became 'A'.

Southern and London Midland and Scottish Railway Companies
SOMERSET AND DORSET JOINT LINE
TO
HIGHBRIDGE.

Chapter Two

Loco Running Sheds (Bath, Templecombe and Wimborne)

Plate 19: A fine view in 1938 from the top of the water softener showing Bath Loco depot with the station in the background.

Author's Collection

This was a wooden structure except for the messroom. Service and cleaning were originally carried out behind closed doors, but these were run into so frequently that they were removed. By the River Avon was the 'boat shed' beside the wharf, used for transfer of goods between rail and barges.

The coal stage was set above the lines to the S&D shed and after coal wagons had been pushed up to the stage, they were unloaded into 10 cwt. tubs by coalmen who then pushed them across the stage and tipped the coal into the tenders of engines standing below. The two-road stone-built MR running shed was situated nearer Bath Queen Square station.

The office and stores block at the S&D shed were built piecemeal. The timber was obtained from Highbridge for 'wagon repairs' and kept until sufficient for some part of the building to be erected. The chimney was built with locomotive brick arch firebricks, while the gas lamps came second hand from Highbridge Works. Water sometimes blocked the gas pipes and the staff had to work by alternative lighting — tallow and wax candles, oil, acetylene

Plate 20: The Railwaymen's Hostel at Wimborne depicting the splendid brickwork, just at the completion of building, showing workman and hostel staff.

R. Atthill Collection

and electric cycle lamps and boilermakers' acetylene flare lamps were all used.

The wooden running shed was approximately 300 ft by 60 ft covering four parallel sets of rails which ended at immense wooden stop blocks. About 10 or 12 wood columns carried the timber beams under the roof centre and each track had a pit the length of the shed. Artificial lighting progressed from tallow candles to portable oil 'duck' lamps (they looked like ducks), gas flame jets and fan gas Bray burners, gas mantle burners and, for the final five years, electricity was used.

Fire precautions consisted of boiler washing-out hoses and numerous buckets of water hanging on the shed walls. Attached to the north-west side of the shed was a machine and fitting shop.

The sidings known as 'Up 7, 8 and 9' just grew and grew, as and when materials became available. The foundations were ashes from the drop pits. Sleepers, rails etc. were obtained from the Engineer's Dept. — paid for by exchange of drivers' and firemen's second hand overcoats which were later distributed to gangers and packers — all unofficially.

Plan of Bath Locomotive Depot.

In 1928, supervision of the former Midland depot was put under the control of the S&D superintendent. The staff still used the old MR depot, but signed on and off at the S&D office. After 1st January, 1930, the MR running shed was reserved for engines under extended repairs.

Templecombe Loco Depot

In the late 1920s, a scheme was proposed for Templecombe to become the depot for the whole of the S&D, with Bath, Bournemouth and Highbridge merely 'garages' in which to stable engines necessary to commence workings. It was envisaged that some of the Southern Railway Salisbury and Yeovil depots' work would also have been undertaken. This idea would have led to great economy, cutting motive power costs by nearly 50 per cent. Movement of staff was the snag as no accommodation in the Templecombe area was available.

One local character at Templecombe was a driver named George, but he was always referred to as 'Gossel' since purchasing some goslings at Wimborne and carrying them home to Templecombe swimming in the tender tank. He always carried a gun on his engine and would shoot any game in sight, stopping his train to retrieve it. He travelled to work by donkey cart, drove it on the turntable, turned it round, and his donkey would return home with the cart alone. It was said that the donkey was bought at Wimborne, hobbled and carried to Templecombe on the tender of Gossel's engine.

During the 1939-45 war, LNER engine No. 8549 and LNER crew were stabled at Templecombe. Permanently in steam and attached to an ambulance train, it was always ready to move at a moment's notice.

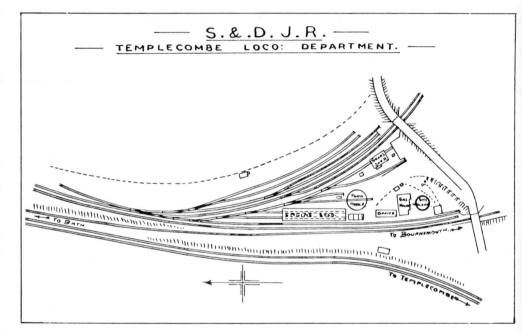

Plan of Templecombe Locomotive Depot.

Wimborne Loco Depot

This was an important depot in the early days, when all trains had to reverse there. The staff lodging house had a resident steward who catered for the trainmen of the many lodging turns of duty which were worked there. The lodging house closed on 1st December, 1922, the lodging house steward being transferred to Branksome as steam-raiser. The shed was closed on 22nd January, 1923, the driver and fireman being transferred to Templecombe; the passed cleaner to Bath; the pumper to Blandford and the district foreman to Templecombe — he was already in charge of Wimborne, Branksome and Templecombe depots. The turntable at Wimborne was last used on 6th July, 1931 and the track from Corfe Mullen Junction to Wimborne was closed for lifting at 4.00 a.m. on 18th June, 1933.

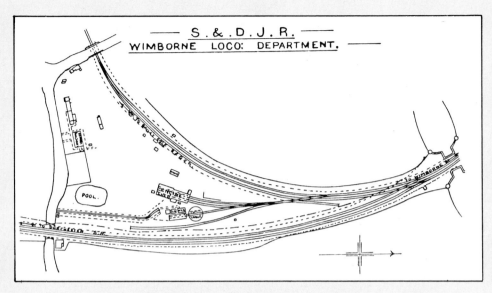

Plan of Wimborne Locomotive Depot.

Plan of Bridgwater Locomotive Depot.

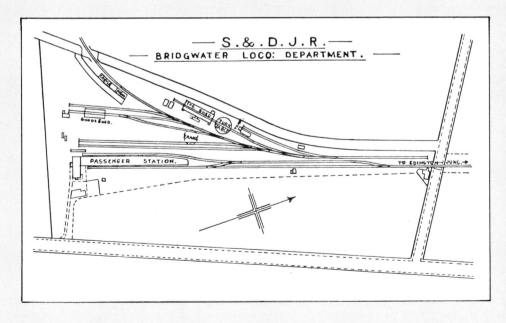

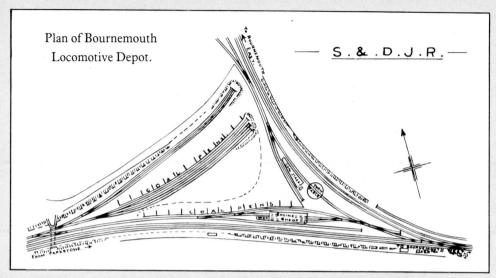

Plan of Bournemouth Locomotive Depot.

S. & . D . J . R .

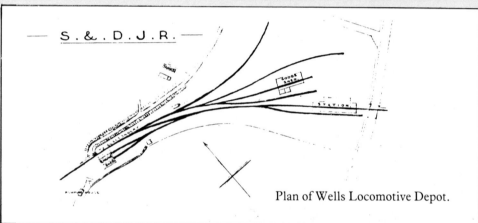

S. & . D . J . R .

Plan of Wells Locomotive Depot.

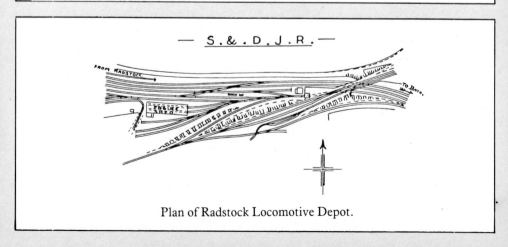

S. & . D . J . R .

Plan of Radstock Locomotive Depot.

Chapter Three

Staff Duties

The work expected of S&D employees was very varied; here are details of the main grades involved:-

Enginemen usually progressed from bar boy or call boy to cleaner; passed cleaner; fireman; passed fireman and then driver.

Bar boys were assistants to bar men who were responsible for cleaning tube plates, brick arches and fire boxes and assisting in renewing the grate firebars.

Call boys were lads used to 'call up' employees, chiefly train staffs, to ensure the attendances at the times required, especially during the night.

Cleaners cleaned the locomotives and were sometimes called on to assist in the sheds on all kinds of duties, especiallly in later years. At one time the engine crew consisted of driver, fireman and cleaner. Often the cleaner met the engine on arrival at the shed and worked on cleaning it for the next turn of duty until the driver took over for that turn.

Firemen saw that tools were correctly positioned on the engine with coal and water aboard and lamps in proper order; the boiler water level was correct and water feeds all working. He fired the engine to maintain steam, kept a lookout for any and every signal and was at the beck and call of the driver. He dropped the fire and cleaned out the smoke box ashes at the disposal of engine after duty was completed.

The Driver's duties were controlled (from signing on to signing off) by the company's rule book and appendix. Before taking charge of his engine the driver obtained copies of notices affecting his particular route and signals, any engineering advice or other work; of crossing of the lines by huntsmen or hounds, lineside slips, water supply notices, any special instructions regarding his train or any other train which might have a bearing on the running of his own train. He would then check to see that any report regarding repairs or adjustment to his own engine had been attended to and, before leaving the shed, assure himself that the engine was in the necessary order to carry out the work required of it. Movements outside the shed signal were controlled by the traffic department, but the driver was required to decide the load. He was responsible for the work done by his fireman and was expected to verify any signals his fireman transmitted to him. On a single line he had to confirm that the tablet or key for the section was the correct one. After the turn of duty ended, he had to report any incidents during the duty, repairs required to his locomotive, (unless previously relieved), and lastly sign off duty.

Messenger; he was a uniformed member of the Works staff at Highbridge who came on duty at 5.00 a.m. and cleaned all the offices; he met trains to give and receive correspondence, and was generally a much wanted man.

Wagon builders were specialist carpenters who constructed the underframes and bodies of wagons.

Bodymakers were the builders of coaches, horse boxes, carriage trucks, parcel vans, milk vans and any coaching stock.

Painters were generally confined to engines, coaches or wagons and did not often change from one type to another. One painter was always engaged in lettering and applying gold leaf.

Carpenters: there were two of these and they made wheelbarrows, sack trucks, sprags etc. for use in the Works, stations and depots.

The *smiths'* shop housed the steam hammer and was chiefly used by a smith with two mates or strikers. Others in the shop were experts at chain making, wagon or carriage fittings — trunions, couplings, buffers etc.

Springsmiths were housed in a separate smithy where one was engaged with the case hardening furnace. One or two were expert in cold sawing ironwork with a circular saw.

Some *labourers* were allocated to particular jobs such as sweeping the Works yard or shops, while others formed a gang, used around the Works for loading and unloading materials. Craftsman assistants were generally known as labourers, but worked with fitters, moulders, boilersmiths etc.

Boilerwashers cleaned the deposits from engine boiler barrels, attended to the blowing down of steam, the cooling of boilers, washing out and refill of boilers.

The tinman made and repaired any tinware required — oil cans, duck lamps, engine lamps, hand lamps etc., oil feeders, buckets and trays of all descriptions.

Turners: it was remarkable how these people turned articles on the old lathes to such fine limits: metal bearings for axle boxes and engine motion gear etc.

Fitters did work of great variety and to fine limits, anything from lineside and engine tablet apparatus, to peg clocks i.e. any metal fitting job.

Patternmakers were the most intriguing of all the craftsmen as everything they did was inside out. They really knew how to work with wood and prepare masters to be used in casting.

The coppersmith was the expert at bending copper and brass piping for all manner of things on steam engines, ships etc., brazing where necessary and running metal into bearings as required.

Boilermakers originally marked out flat steel and copper plates and bent and made them into locomotive boilers. In later years they were chiefly engaged as riveters on repairs to boilers etc.

Vacuum brake examiners tested coaching stock vacuum brake gear and replaced or repaired faulty cylinders, pistons, rubber rings and adjusted operating gear as necessary.

Carriage fitters and assistants fitted ironwork to coach and wagon frames.

The carriage maker made the drays etc. which carried goods around the various towns from the railway stations at, amongst others, Glastonbury, Wells, Wincanton, Blandford, Shepton Mallet, Highbridge and Burnham.

The driller chiefly operated drilling machines, but was often found at the controls of a grinder or shaping machine.

The gas fitter was also the electrician working on coaching vehicles plus also being the Works plumber etc.

The examiner was a Carriage & Wagon Dept. employee. His duties covering the examination of vehicles and their components, e.g. tyres, couplings, buffers, springs, brake gear, lighting, door fittings etc. Wheel tapping gave indication of faults in wheels, tyres and axles. He put 'Not To Go' labels on vehicles and decided when it was safe to remove them.

The greaser filled the grease axle boxes with lubricant and assisted lifters and examiners when required.

Chapter Four

Water Supply

Nothing matters more to a steam locomotive than water. Even coal is often easier to come by. Here is how water was made available at the various depots on the Somerset and Dorset:-

Bath — gravity from Devonshire Tunnel; electric pump and city mains.
Radstock — town water.
Chilcompton — steam- (later petrol-) driven pump.
Shepton Mallet — town mains.
Evercreech Junction — steam- (later petrol-) driven pump.
Templecombe — town mains.
Sturminster Newton — town mains.
Blandford — steam pump, later electric motor pump.
Branksome — town mains.
Bournemouth — town mains.
Glastonbury — steam-, later petrol- (later electric-) driven pump.
Wells — water wheel.
Bridgwater — town mains.
Highbridge — steam- (later electric-) driven pump, town mains.
Burnham — town mains.
Wimborne — steam pump.

Bath: during the excavation of Devonshire Tunnel springs were tapped and led into a sump at the tunnel entrance at the Bath end. Both 4 in. and 6 in. pipes carried the water by gravity to a tank at the Bath Loco Depot. Additionally a well was sunk near the boat shed on the bank of the Avon from which a two-throw ram pump (normal revs. 112 per min.) transferred water into a 30,000 gallon tank. A system of valves permitted a number of variations to the direction of flow, but eventually practically all water went through the water softening plant.

Evercreech Junction: the steam pump house was about half a mile down the track towards Cole, on the banks of the tiny River Alham, a tributary of the River Brue. Two pumpers worked shifts of 12 hours each, though latterly there was only one. An electric pump was installed on 21st June, 1942.

One pumper had a fairly large family, and to help feed them, he put down 'wires' to snare rabbits along the railway embankment. This was known to all the enginemen and on at least one occasion, one of them raided the wires, paunched the rabbit and left the remains in the snare for the pumper.

Templecombe: water supplies were a problem for both the LSWR and S&D. Engines stabling at Templecombe were always expected to fill up at the last watering point. The S&D used old tenders, suitably adapted, and these were run over a sump in the track at Templecombe Upper and fed the 25,000 gallon tank in the loco depot below. These travelling tanks were run between Blandford and Shepton Mallet and were usually attached to an ordinary goods train, but occasionally they were made up into purely water trains.

In later years, reliable supplies were piped to Templecombe from Milborne Port, and the S&D erected a 'parachute' tank (2,200 gallons capacity) at Templecombe Upper. The pressure in the loco depot hydrants was so good, that for a time, until a booster pump was installed at Bath depot for washing out, the Class 80 2-8-0 engines' roster was arranged to allow the engines sufficient time at Templecombe shed to enable them to be more efficiently washed out by the pressure available there.

Glastonbury and Highbridge: when tannery effluent at Glastonbury and milk factory effluent and sea water at Highbridge caused boiler priming due to water contamination, travelling water tanks would be used to carry water from Wells and Shepton Mallet. Eight old tenders were allocated to Highbridge for working this service, these being Nos. 1565, 2266, 2337, 2478, 2497, 2599, 2876, and 2980.

Wells: the S&D water tank at Wells had a private pipe connection to supply a farm whose water supply was cut off by the diversion of a stream when the railway branch was built. Crossing-keepers were supplied from Wells by eight gallon cans at regular times, trains being stopped to put off the cans, and also light engines ran from Edington Junction to Chilton Drove Crossing with cans of water.

Wimborne: Charles Osman was engaged as pumper on 15th April, 1877, and because of shortness of work was discharged after more than 45 years service on 19th August, 1922.

WATER RADIUS OF SOMERSET AND DORSET LOCOMOTIVES

Loco Numbers	*Average galls. per mile*	*Tank capacity galls.*	*Water radius miles*
67-71	32.5	3,250	100
10 class	32.4	876	27
52, 53, 55	32.7	950	29
54	33.8	1,150	34
80-85	87.5	3,500	40
86-90	70.0	3,500	50
1-7 & 9	30.9	1,360	44
14-18 & 45	40.0	2,600	65

Chapter Five

Locomotives

Highbridge and the other locomotive depots cannot be considered without reference to the engines which they serviced. The following is not a complete run-down on the S&DJR locomotive stock, but deals with most of the important classes and refers to each by photographs included in the text.

Plate 21 is of No. 1 an 0-6-0ST built 1874 by Fox Walker, and rebuilt December 1908 with saddle-tank extended over smokebox. *Plate 22* shows sister engine No. 2 at Midsomer Norton, with the local staff 'posed' by the stationary engine. These engines were shedded at Bath and Radstock for shunting and banking duties, though in early days they worked the goods trains from Bath to Evercreech Junction and beyond.

Plate 23 was taken at Bath in 1895 and shows 0-6-0ST No. 1 converted to a tender engine (which took place in January 1888).

Plate 24 is of 0-6-0T No.8, built by Fox Walker as a passenger engine; she was constructed in 1876 as a saddle tank, and rebuilt as a side-tank in 1889, being one of a series of nine engines. The photograph was taken at High-

Plate 21: 0-6-0ST No. 1.

Plate 22: 0-6-0ST No. 2 (with crew) at Midsomer Norton.

Plate 23: 0-6-0 No. 1 tender locomotive at Bath c. 1895.

Bath Railway Society

Plate 24: 0-6-0T No. 8

British Rail

bridge Works. No. 8 was very extensively used on passenger trains between Bath and Bournemouth and was the only S&D Fox Walker design fitted for vacuum brake working. In 1908 it was converted into a tender engine, still 'vacuum fitted'. It was used for goods train working and before being sent for scrap in 1928, did duty in the loco shed at Bath as a hot water washing out apparatus, being kept constantly in steam. Injectors transferred steam and water from No. 8 into the boilers for and after washing out. This method of washing out of other engine boilers saved hours of time 'cooling down' and 'warming up' again when washing out became due on boilers. Some cleaners used No. 8 to steam-clean other engines, until a spate of hot bearings resulted from the oil being washed from them.

No. 8 always retained its Fox Walker type of motion gear and, compared with other side tank engines, shows a much smaller coal bunker, i.e. 2-2½ tons. The S&D coat of arms was, in this case, positioned above the number.

Plate 25 Locomotive No. 9 (built Fox Walker 1876) seen here at Bath Loco Depot, came out of Highbridge Works with its saddle tank extended over the smokebox in April 1910. Before economies resulted in the all black livery, these engines appeared in full lining, with polished domes and burnished rods and buffers, and had a distinctive appearance. Each ran over a million miles during their lifetimes.

Plate 26 shows 0-6-0T No. 22, built 1929 (Bagnall Works No. 2361). These engines were shedded at Bath and Radstock and were used for shunting and banking duties, replacing the Fox Walker 0-6-0STs. At first the Bagnalls were used as assisting engines on passenger trains, but their small wheels led them to be banned from this duty by A. H. Whitaker. Mr. Whitaker was the District Locomotive Superintendent at Bath, and the son of the former Locomotive Superintendent. No. 22 was the longest lived S&D engine in BR service, being withdrawn in 1967, and ended her days at Westhouses, Derbyshire.

Plate 25: 0-6-0ST No. 9.

Author's Collection

Plate 26: 0-6-0T No. 22.

Author's Collection

Plate 27: 2-4-0T No. 27A.

Real Photographs

Plate 28 photographed at Highbridge Works in 1899 portrays 2-4-0ST, No. 28A, built by George England in 1861 as a tender engine.

The author understands that it was stationed at Wells and worked the branch and also ran between Burnham and Templecombe. No. 28A and its twin, 27A, *(Plate 27)* were rebuilt as side tanks and worked shifts, shunting at Highbridge Wharf and running the twenty eight short passenger trains between Highbridge and Burnham daily, as well as trips to Glastonbury to carry out shunting duties.

These engines also worked transfer trips to the GWR at Highbridge and between Highbridge Loco Works and Wharf. Both engines had polished axleboxes to the pony truck and reportedly looked smart.

Plate 29 shows 0-4-4T No. 13 built by Avonside in 1877 (Works No. 1188) and photographed here at Highbridge; the number is on the side tank instead of on the bunker; the original practice. This is a representative of a series of engines used extensively on passenger trains, except the local Highbridge-Burnham Branch service. Nos. 10 to 14A were allocated to Highbridge; 52 and 53 to Bridgwater; 54 and 55 to Wells and 29 to 32 to Templecombe. *Plate 30* shows sister locomotive No. 12 at Evercreech Jn. in 1877; all the station staff appear to want to be included in the photograph, as usual! The four engines at Templecombe worked over the main line to Bath and Bournemouth as well as duties over the branches. The engines were 'Class 1' for goods working and served as goods engines when required. Some were fitted for push and pull working — No. 31A was at Templecombe for working to Bournemouth, and No. 52 at Wells.

Loaded weights varied between 43½-51½ tons. Tank sizes also varied, though the general capacity was 876 gallons, but No. 53 was 950 gallons and No. 54 was 1,150 gallons. The bunkers carried a uniform 2 tons 2 cwt. of coal. Rebuilding of the class at Highbridge Works commenced in 1906 with engine No. 13, and in 1910 these engines were allocated to drivers and their names were painted inside the cabs.

Plates 31 and 32 show the colliery shunter No. 25A, an 0-4-2ST built at Highbridge in 1885, and photographed at Radstock before its 1897 rebuild. The engine cab had a roof extending from firebox to buffer beam with an interior bunker for coal. The handbrake crank handle shows above the bunker. Nos. 25A, 26A and 45A were specially constructed engines for working the Clandown Colliery branch, shunting in Radstock goods yard, working Writhlington and Braysdown Colliery sidings, and passing through the 'Marble Arch', a low bridge leading to the level crossing on the A 362 Radstock-Frome road. A colliery tip line ran over the bridge, taking waste from Tyning Colliery. These three engines were known as 'Dazzlers', 'Jinties' or 'Jockers'.

Plate 33 portrays an 0-4-0ST No. 45A, as rebuilt at Highbridge from an 0-4-0ST 'Bristol' in 1895, and pictured here at Radstock. The engine appears

Plate 28: 2-4-0T No. 28A.

Plate 29: 0-4-4T No. 13.

Plate 30: 0-4-4T No. 12 at Evercreech Junction with crew.

Bath Railway Society

Plate 31: 0-4-2T No. 25A.

Author's Collection

Plate 32: 0-4-2T No. 25A at Radstock.

Author's Collection

Plate 33: 0-4-0T No. 45A.

Author's Collection

fresh from shops, as paintwork, handrails and motion are very clean (note the underslung crosshead). The cylinder lubricator is above the raised footplate and piston rod lubricator on the front top of the slide bar. Coal was carried in the side bunkers, and tools on the floor of the cab. The brake rod runs under the firebox. She was withdrawn from service in 1929.

Plate 34 is of an 0-6-0 No. 20, built in 1874 by Fowler (Works No. 2126), and photographed at Highbridge Works. In the early days tenders were not lettered, but 'SDJR' appeared on the front buffer beam. It is believed that no engine of this class appeared at Bath after 1922. On at least one occasion, a Fowler hauling an up train through Combe Down tunnel started slipping, and the weight of the train dragged it back through the tunnel entrance it had just passed.

Plate 35 This interesting period piece shows No. 23 on a goods train at Blandform Forum. The engine is in immaculate condition, as were many of the S&D locomotives in their heyday.

Plate 36 is of an 0-6-0 No. 46, built by Vulcan in 1884 (Works No. 1055). This class of general-purpose engines were known as 'Scotties', as the first batch (Nos. 33 to 38) were built by Neilson, Reid & Co. of Glasgow. The engine and tender weighed about 65 tons and was rated as Class 1 for loading purposes. There were 28 of these engines and their work took them to every part of the S&D system, and on every class of job, from shunting to express passenger. S&D practice considered an engine and tender as one, and it was not until the LMS take-over that the tenders carried a number of their own. Locomotives Nos. 27 and 28 were at one time fitted with a cab on the tender for tender-first working from Templecombe Upper to Highbridge. This was to work the empty milk churn train, after coming off the loaded milk train for London (Vauxhall) at Templecombe Upper and eliminated the delay caused by having to run to the Lower Yard to turn.

One summer day, about 1910, No. 25 ran once on a Barry Railway boat excursion, non-stop from Burnham to Poole. Coal capacity of the tender was normally 3 tons and 2,200 gallons of water. Since the average consumption of water on passenger trains was 30 gallons per mile, Driver F. Milton and Fireman F. Kemery of Higbridge must have had great confidence in their engine to contemplate running approximately 70 miles into Bournemouth West with possibly only 100 gallons left in the tank.

Plate 37 is of No. 35 at Templecombe Upper. Just visible are the signal-man's two observation catwalks. Churns stand on the platform, and a milk van can be seen on the right of the photograph, with the LSWR main line to Waterloo running beyond.

Plate 38 shows 0-6-0 No. 38, built by Vulcan in 1890 (Works No. 1269). This picture was probably taken after the rebuilding in 1928. These engines were very similar to the Neilson & Co. Nos. 72-6, but were smaller, with the G5 instead of G7 boilers giving less heating surface, 10 lb. less pressure, smaller cylinders and tenders. No. 38 was allocated to Highbridge depot,

Plate 34: 0-6-0 No. 20.

British Rail

Plate 35: 0-6-0 No. 23 at Blandford.

L.G.R.P. Courtesy David and Charles

Plate 36: 0-6-0 No. 46.

Plate 37: 0-6-0 No. 35 at Templecombe.

Plate 38: 0-6-0 No. 38.

working the goods traffic to Evercreech Junction and remaining there 'round the clock', shunting at Evercreech Junction North, banking goods trains and assisting passenger trains from Evercreech Junction to Binegar. When 4-4-0s Nos. 15 and 16 were scrapped, Nos. 34 and 35 were given their tenders, increasing their water capacity from 2,200 to 2,600 gallons. This gave these engines an advantage of 13 miles extra travel, or a slight increase in loading.

Plate 39 shows 0-6-0 No. 58, built in 1890 by Vulcan (Works No. 1266); a similar engine to Nos. 46 and 56, but all safety valves are over the firebox and the cover was elliptical. A peculiarity of some of these engines was that the leading and trailing journals were conical 7½ in. diameter at the end and 6½ in. at the centre. No. 59 of this class had a broken frame and ended its days as the Glastonbury Yard shunter. In the 1920s it ran light to and from Glastonbury (ex-Highbridge) and its 'rattle-bang-clatter' could be heard for miles around.

Plate 40 is of an 0-6-0, No. 60, built by the Armstrong Whitworth Co. in 1922 (Works No. 471). Although classified as a freight engine, it was really a mixed-traffic locomotive and was almost as much at ease working an express passenger train as hauling a ballast train or shunting. When working a passenger train, its permitted load was only exceeded by Class 5, 4-6-0s and the S&D 80 class — 365 tons against 405 and 450 tons respectively.

Plate 41 shows an 0-6-0, No. 57, standing by Highbridge weighbridge.

Plate 42 depicts a small 4-4-0, No. 15, at Bournemouth West. Built at Derby in 1891, it was reboilered in 1910 with the Johnson 'H' pattern. To accommodate the larger boiler, the frames were lengthened behind the trailing coupled wheels, with the cab roof being extended backwards also.

Plate 43 is of a 4-4-0, No. 70, built at Derby in 1903. The dimensions were larger than the earlier Johnson 4-4-0s and this engine was rather more capable of working S&D passenger services. Attractive features of No. 70 were the three safety valves in a large brass casing over the firebox, curved brass beading above the splashers and a wheel fastening the smokebox door. Features new to S&D engines included fluted coupling rods and strap type smokebox door hinges.

No. 71, a 4-4-0, is seen *(Plate 44)* in World War I (next to a tidy coal stack at Bath Depot) with women cleaners and young cleaning lads. Note the livery of the lettering on the buffer beam.

Plate 45 is of a 4-4-0 No. 78 express passenger (3P 2G) built in 1907 at Derby, standing on No. 9 road at Bath Depot. No. 78 appears to be in the condition in which it came from Highbridge Works after rebuilding in November 1921 having rivet heads showing on the smokebox; on the sister engine No. 77, they were flush.

No. 78 was a Deeley version of the same type as No. 70 but with modified cab, smokebox door secured by clips and bolts and no brass beading to the splashers.

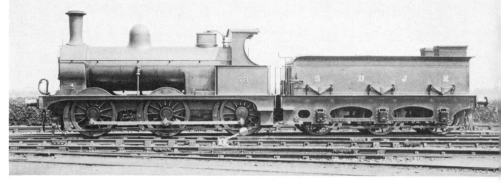

Plate 39: 0-6-0 No. 58.

Author's Collection

Plate 40: 0-6-0 No. 60.

Author's Collection

Plate 41: 0-6-0 No. 57 at Highbridge.

Author's Collection

Plate 42: 4-4-0 No. 15 at Bournemouth West.

Bath Railway Society

Plate 43: 4-4-0 No. 70.

R. Andrews Collection

Plate 44: 4-4-0 No. 71 at Bath; women cleaners in World War I.

Author's Collection

Plate 45: 4-4-0 No. 78 at Bath.

Author's Collection

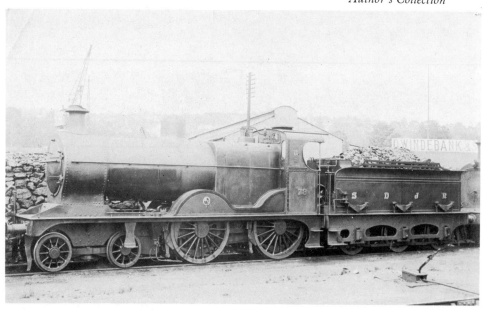

Plates 46, 47 and 48 depict the 2-8-0 '80' class. These engines arrived on the S&D as follows: Nos. 80 and 81 February 1914, Nos. 82 and 83 March 1914, No. 84 April 1914, No. 85 July 1914. First classified '5', they were altered to '7' in 1930. These engines, when received, were fitted with tender cabs to assist tender-first working. They had steam reversing gear, steam sanding and brakes on the front and rear of the leading pony truck. The tender cabs, steam reverse gear, steam sanding and brakes on the pony trucks were removed about 1918 and dry sanding, and hand-winding reverse gear replacing all the original fitments. The tender cabs were said to cause an unpleasant draught. When the engines arrived, the deflector lip at the front of the chimney was too near the arch of Devonshire and Combe Down tunnels and was removed to reduce the height to 13 ft 3 in. Dust from the cast iron brake blocks caused wear on the slide bars motion and cylinders, which led to a trial of Ferodo brake blocks on the leading wheels of No. 13801 in November 1943. Later, all wheels on this engine were fitted with Ferodo blocks which proved so successful that they were fitted on all the engines of the class. Cast iron brake blocks had to be replaced after a trip of about 52 miles (Bath-Evercreech Junction and back), but Ferodo blocks lasted approximately 4 weeks, were much easier to fit as they were lighter and eliminated wear on the slide bars. Drivers could pull up so well with the Ferodo brake blocks that the practice of pinning down brakes ceased. Drivers claimed that descending steep gradients, the cast iron blocks grew so incandescent they could see across two fields at night!

The first time an engine of this class worked a passenger train was about 1924, when there was a shortage of engines. It ran from Bath to Bournemouth in 'Pines Express' timing.

When the '80' class first came to the S&D, their size and weight so restricted their operation that they were confined to working between Radstock and Evercreech Junction only. Bridges and culverts all along the line had to be strengthened and it was some time before they could work into Templecombe. As they were stationed at Radstock running shed, men had to travel from Bath to man the engines and clean them. For a long time there was only one turntable on which they could be turned, their wheelbase of 50 ft 1 in.just scraping round on the 50 ft turntable at Templecombe. Later, Evercreech Junction North had a 56 ft table and Bath Loco a 60 ft 2 in. table, and when running into Bournemouth there were no difficulties, as they could be turned on the triangle. Eventually the whole line was strengthened, and although speed and load limits existed, it was no longer necessary to empty the boiler and tender tank, remove coal and stack the side and piston rods on the tender to make it possible to run to Highbridge Works or Bath Loco Depot for repairs.

The load restrictions varied between 17 and 66 wagons, depending on the route, make-up of train, and whether a banker was rendering assistance. For

Plate 46: 2-8-0 No. 80 at Derby Works.

British Rail

Plate 47: 2-8-0 No. 84, tender cab removed.

Author's Collection

Plate 48: 2-8-0 No. 90.

Author's Collection

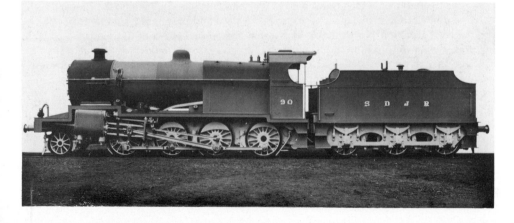

example, 17 wagons were a single load from Bath to Midford or Radstock to Moorewood, and Evercreech Junction to Binegar, but when the load of an '80' class engine contained not more than 5 wagons of mineral, the train could be made equal to 80 quarters. To arrive at this alternative loading, wagons were equated as follows:

$$
\begin{aligned}
\text{one empty} &= 2 \text{ quarters} \\
\text{one goods} &= 3 \text{ quarters} \\
\text{one 8 ton mineral} &= 4 \text{ quarters} \\
\text{one 10 ton mineral} &= 5 \text{ quarters} \\
\text{one 12 ton mineral} &= 6 \text{ quarters}
\end{aligned}
$$

The first engines acquitted themselves so successfully that a further five were ordered. These later ones had larger diameter boilers and carried 1½ tons less coal. No. 90 is illustrated in *Plate 48*.

Plate 49 shows Sentinel Steam Shunting Engine No. 102. Nos. 101 and 102 were the last engines to be supplied new to the S&D. Built in 1929, they replaced Nos. 25A, 26A and 45A as Radstock Colliery shunting engines and were specially designed to pass through the low 'Marble Arch'. They had vertical boilers situated in the cab and wheels were coupled by a chain, the gear ratio being 3.929 to 1. The square spectacle windows were of ample size

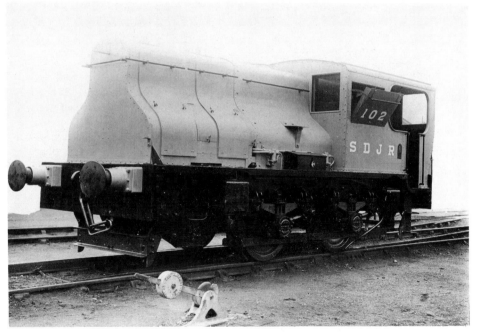

Plate 49: 0-4-0 Sentinel Locomotive No. 102 in works grey livery.
Author's Collection

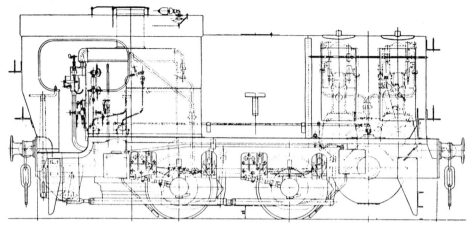

200 H.P. SENTINEL SHUNTING LOCOMOTIVE, SOMERSET & DORSET JOINT RY.

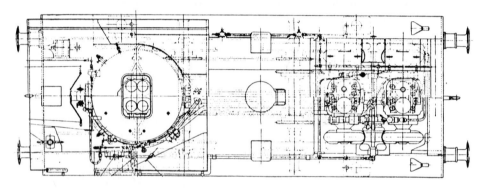

to give a good view. The side flap on the cab was a coal chute and the tool box was on the running plate. This view is probably the final Highbridge Works photograph taken by Samuel Wyatt of Burnham and was photographed near the crossing by the gas fitters's shop.

The intention was for these locomotives to be worked by only one engine-man, but in the event they were always crewed by two. They spent all their lives at Radstock; running repairs and examination being carried out by the fitter at Radstock who was originally responsible for them being kept in good order. They made occasional visits to the Bath shed for repair.

'Foreign' engines sometimes appeared on the S&D. In 1906, LSWR K11 class rail motor No. 1 was loaned to the S&D for trials between Highbridge and Burnham, but was found to be quite incapable of handling the heavy summer traffic as extra coaches could not be added when required. It did not compare with Nos. 27A and 28A for economical working, since it could not also be used for shunting in between trips. About 1912, Midland Railway 0-6-4T No. 2023 was loaned to the S&D. At one time there was talk of using a Garratt on the 'Pines Express', but it was rumoured that the axle load prevented its use.

Chapter Six

The Whitaker Tablet Exchanging Apparatus

Plates 50 to 54. In the days prior to mechanical exchanges, firemen collected newspapers out of the coaches to make pads around their arms and at their backs, to cut down the bruising sustained when picking up the tablet pouches. One paper — one pick-up at most speeds; the tablet split a halfpenny paper in half!

Alfred Whitaker patented his tablet changing apparatus in 1905 and in May 1907 a fitter was specially employed for work on this project. The apparatus was tested at Highbridge where a specially long sleeper was put in the track for the lineside apparatus to be bolted to. Usually No. 25, a 'Scottie' 0-6-0 tender engine, carried the locomotive equipment. The engine would quickly accelerate from the 'Burnham' platform at Highbridge stop block, to make tests.

The normal type of exchange apparatus was turned at right angles to the track in order to make a catch, the impact on collection turning the arm away from the train in order to give the necessary safety margin of clearance. In places where space was very limited (such as between tracks) a different type of apparatus was used. In this alternative pattern, the impact of collection swung the apparatus into a sump, completely out of reach of passing trains and thus ensuring safety. This type of apparatus was picturesquely known as the 'falling man'.

A 'falling man' was situated at Templecombe No. 2 Junction signalbox and also at Corfe Mullen Junction. When S&D trains ceased running to Wimborne, the Corfe Mullen Junction apparatus was re-erected at Bath Junction to collect the tablet from engines passing on the goods line. On the Highbridge branch, exchanging the tablet was always by hand.

The Bagnall side tanks were fitted with a 'slot' bolted to the cab side and this plate enabled a 'Woolworth' (the slang name for a catcher) to be put into position to make a catch from the Binegar Station pillar, when banking, so that it could return on the wrong line from Masbury summit.

On one occasion, two Armstrong class 4F 0-6-0 locomotives were coupled at the head of a full load from Chilcompton while a Bagnall was banking at the rear. Being a double line the Binegar banking key was put out for the banker only, but the fireman on the leading engine, looking ahead and seeing the key in the station apparatus, put out his own catcher and remarked 'I got'n mate'. It was the only time the inspector on the engine was known to swear, and his 'You b . . . . . fool', although immediately followed with 'I am sorry', was really from the bottom of his heart. The key was thrown off the engine to be lost for hours, and the banker dropped off at Binegar, leaving the train to crawl over Masbury summit without banking assistance.

Plate 50: An autographed photograph of A. Whitaker, dated 22nd July, 1911.

Author's Collection

Plate 51: The single line tablet exchange taking place at Midford, in pre-Whitaker Tablet Exchanging apparatus days. Approaching with an up train is an 0-4-4T.

R. Andrews Collection

Plate 52: Shows the tablet catcher, retracted in the travelling position.

Bath Railway Society

Plate 53: The tablet catcher in the extended position. Photographed at the moment of collection and delivery.

Bath Railway Society

Plate 54: A close-up of the 'falling man' type of tablet catcher seen here laying prone having caught the tablet at Templecombe No. 2 Junction in 1906.

Author's Collection

Until 1929, it is believed, banking engines were coupled to the goods brake van and ran through to Masbury. Goods brake vans were then fitted with special hooks to uncouple the banking engine on the wrong line protected by the banking key issued at Binegar. In later years, a rack for carrying a shunter's pole was kept on the front of a banker so that the guard could just lean out to uncouple.

Chapter Seven

Snow Ploughs

The snow ploughs were originally made to fit the Fox Walker saddle-tank engines, and were altered when the saddle tanks were rebuilt, then altered once more to fit the Bagnall tanks. Two ploughs were kept at Bath and used for the front and rear of an 0-6-0T and two at Highbridge for front and rear of an 0-4-4T. After control of the S&D passed to Derby, an inventory of all machinery, hand tools, plant and equipment was called for. The list from the Bath return included a pair of snow ploughs for the Bagnall tank engines. Derby headquarters informed them that there were no snow ploughs south of Derby. The S&D reply from Bath was that not only did they have and regularly use them, but that there was also a pair at Highbridge. Apparently the people at Highbridge did not recognize them as snow ploughs, and thought they were scrap metal, while the people who knew what they were had forgotten about them as they had become overgrown at the back of the shed. The Bath depot snow ploughs were finally adapted for use on the still more powerful Armstrong class 4F 0-6-0 locomotives, but even they were known to become stuck in the deep drifts on Mendip Hills.

Chapter Eight

Carriage Stock

The more modern S&D carriages were fairly familiar; many of them continued to run in Southern Railway livery until the time of the last War. The coaches described here may not be so well-known.

Plate 55 shows a First Class 4-wheel Coach No. 1, at Highbridge. This coach is similar to First Class No. 4, smashed in the Binegar collision of 1885. (The scroll on the panel from this crash with '4' in the centre, hung on

Plate 55: Coach No. 1.   *Author's Collection*

Plate 56: Coach No. 6.

Author's Collection

Plate 57: Coach No. 12.

Author's Collection

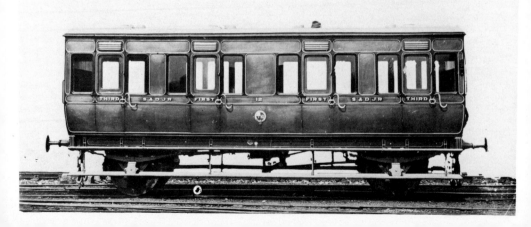

the wall behind the desk of the chief foreman of the Carriage and Wagon Department).

No. 1 had safety chains and screw couplings; the smoking compartment was on the left (in those days there were special compartments for smoking, not for non-smoking). A white star on the underframe marked the position of the 'string' pull to destroy the vacuum, releasing the brakes and thus moving in an unfitted train.

Plate 56 shows Third Class Coach No. 6, at Highbridge. Similar in size to No. 1, it was divided into four instead of three compartments. The match-board partitions were painted and grained and seats were thin removable horsehair stuffed cushions. Pre-heated sealed footwarmers were used; a special furnace at Highbridge station boiled water to heat these containers.

Plate 57 shows Coach No. 12 with the 1st-class compartments positioned in the centre, for comfort. Note width of centre panel and very narrow end panels. Window blinds in the 1st-class compartments were of horsehair weft, and ceilings of embossed lincrusta; the 3rd-class merely had painted match-board. It was very smart, with polished brass door handles and step strips; even the underframe was lined.

Plate 58 shows Composite Coach No. 20. This coach, replacing an older 4-wheeled vehicle, had two first and two third-class compartments with centre luggage compartment. Gas lighting was from a cylinder beneath the coach and the pressure gauge shows on the underframe below the right hand window of the left hand first-class compartment. Note the S&D crest on first-class doors.

Plate 58: Coach No. 20.

British Rail

Plate 59: Coach No. 33.

Author's Collection

Plate 60: Coach No. 52.

Author's Collection

Plate 61: Coach No. 100.

British Rail

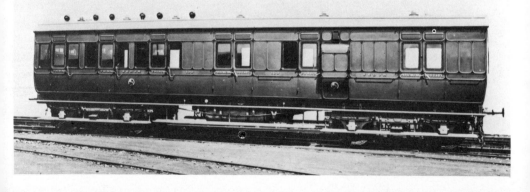

Plate 59 is of a Brake Third Coach No. 33 at Highbridge. There is vertical matchboard panelling in the right hand compartment and horizontal parcelling in the other. The coach is standing on flat-bottomed rail.

Plate 60 shows a Third Class Coach No. 52 built by the Oldbury Carriage Company and seen here at Highbridge. The second and fourth compartments have vertical boarding and the others, horizontal. The star on the solebar below the coach number indicates the position of the brake release chain. Similar to coach No. 20, it was entirely third class and had no central luggage compartment and was oil lit.

Plate 61 shows a Brake Third Coach No. 100 seen again at Highbridge. The guard's compartment with lookout ducket was flanked on either side by a compartment for Passengers' Luggage, access being through double doors.

Plate 62 portrays a workmen's train set comprising coaches Nos. 1, 2 & 3 *(right to left)* photographed at Highbridge Works. Labelled *To run between Highbridge & Burnham only*, this set was close-coupled and tight buffered, and only used for workmen. The ordinary fare was 1½d. each way, but a workman's ticket, (issued in the Works) cost men 6d. and boys 3d. per week. The guard was a painter paid 24s. per week for 54 hours work, who had an allowance of 1s. 6d. per week for acting as guard — but still had to pay 6d. for his workman's ticket! These vehicles were ex-regular service coaches and the end compartment (near part of the weighbridge house on the right) was the only upholstered compartment on the train. This was reserved for the use of the supervisory and clerical staff who travelled free. The guard's seats at each end were probably cushioned and part padded while all others were painted matchboard. The men always alighted at Highbridge station platform and walked along the track (in all weathers) but joined it at the Loco Works from ground level near the mess room, when travelling home. The end of the weighhouse shown in the picture was the dark room for blue prints and the large zinc bath used for washing prints, was also used by office boys for hot baths in winter and cold dips in warmer weather. It was easy to get hot water from the nearby mess room and this luxury of bathing was a boon to boys not living at home and it is believed that their superiors never 'rumbled' them.

Plate 62: Workmen's coaches Nos. 1-3.

Author's Collection

Chapter Nine

Goods Stock

The study of goods rolling stock has only recently come to the fore and was for many years a neglected but important area of railway history. The following examples are typical of a railway at the turn of the century.

Plate 63 is of a goods brake van No. 6 weighing 20 t. 5 cwt. 3 qr. Known as 'mail vans' they were used on the 2.40 a.m. mail goods train from Bath to Bournemouth for carrying Royal Mail. Although a goods vehicle, it was built by the carriage bodymakers (not wagon builders) and a number of carriage fittings were incorporated — doors fitted with carriage locks and windows, oil lamps built into roof. Cast iron slabs were fitted to the underframe to make up weight and hand operated brake gear applied to front and rear of all six wheels.

The S&D appendix is believed to be the only one in the country which gave detailed instructions to drivers and guards of freight trains; where, when and how to operate engine and guard's brakes effectively and to control trains on its steep gradients.

Plate 63: Brake Van No. 6.

Author's Collection

Plate 64 shows also a goods brake van No. 34 but weighing only 10 t. 12 cwt. 0 qr. The axles, wheels and tyres were made by specialist contractors or the Midland Railway. Timber passed through the sawmill at Highbridge and oak or similar hard wood was used for the underframe with ash for the body frame and matchboard top and sides. Pine was used for the floor and the roof was covered by canvas which was glued on. Blacksmiths made the iron-work; springsmiths the spring gear; moulders cast the iron and brass castings from patterns made by the patternmaker, while apprentice boilersmiths did the rivet work and the machine shop drilled the ironwork. Actual construc-tion was by the wagon builders. Body and frame were bolted directly to-gether, whereas coaching stock were insulated with rubber pads made by Spencer Moulton, Melksham. Cast iron weight blocks filled the underframes and to give extra braking power, guards sometimes used a bar for leverage on the brake handle. In later years the vans were fitted with dry sand boxes to increase adhesion when loads became heavier in the 1920s. The finished van was painted grey with black iron work and the word 'tare' was usually painted on the bottom body rail at the door end and sometimes carved at the opposite end, or branded into the rail. Numbers, as well as being near the roof, were painted along the bottom rail and also appeared on the maker's plate. The white patch on the front end of the van was for marking the latest date of lifting, oiling or greasing, or other running repairs. Handrails were all solid bars and all brake vans were fitted with cast iron coal fired stoves, cast in the moulding shop.

Plate 64: Brake Van No. 34.

Author's Collection

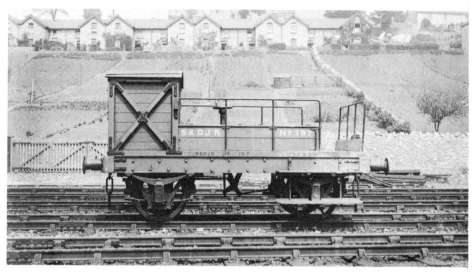

Plate 65: Brake Van No. 197.

Plate 66: Double bolster No. 71.

Plate 67: Single bolster No. 118.

Plate 65 is another goods brake van No. 197 weighing this time 7 t. 11 cwt. 2 qr. Pictured here at Radstock probably in spring of 1905; built at Highbridge in 1889 and constructed specially to pass under the low 'Marble Arch' at Radstock, it was used for working trips from Radstock Goods Yard and sidings at Writhlington, Braysdown and Clandown branch. The brake standard, wheel and handle were situated in the open part of the van.

Plate 66 portrays a double bolster wagon No. 71, tare 6 t. 14 cwt. 2 qr, with a load capacity of 10 tons. Built c. 1904, it was a sign of an increase in loading requirements leading to a longer wagon for cheaper carriage charges than the single bolster wagons in those competitive days. Of slightly increased weight, it transported roughly 2 wagon loads and was fitted with spring draw and buffing gear and oil axle boxes.

Plate 67 shows a single bolster wagon No. 118 photographed at Highbridge around 1900. This dumb buffered wagon with grease axle boxes, was used for carrying rails, timber, logs and other long loads. A cast iron plate in the centre of the plank bears the wagon number and building date, 1886. The brake gear was only fitted to one side, that nearest the camera. On the left a 'Jim Crow' leans against a stone.

Plate 68 is of coupled bolster wagons Nos. 374 & 366. This type operated in pairs having a curved buffer bar in the centre at one end, linked to a twin on the other wagon by means of a drop pin. The other end had normal buffers, hook and three link coupling. Although the coupling arrangement caused the wagons to work in pairs, it was not essential for the same two to be used together. It should be noted that these wagons by being fitted with brake gear on one side only, gave the shunting staff only half the maximum brake power on two wagons, unless they walked down each side. This also applied to trains which had to stop and pin down brakes before descending some of the 1 in 50 gradients on the S&D.

Plate 68: Twin single bolster Nos. 374/366.

Author's Collection

Plate 69: Carriage wagon No. 641.
Author's Collection

Plate 70: Wagon No. 141.

Author's Collection

Plate 71: Wagon No. 174.

Author's Collection

Plate 72: Wagon No. 210.

Author's Collection

Plate 69 shows a carriage truck No. 641, tare 7 t. 12 cwt. 2 qr. This type of wagon was used for transporting road vehicles, such as horse-drawn carriages, carts and farm wagons, but also steam road rollers from Lodge of Shepton Mallet, Edison of Dorchester and Buncombe of Highbridge. It was end loading, with cast iron brake blocks and lettered *To be returned to Glastonbury.*

Plate 70 shows a five-plank high-sided wagon No. 141, built 1886 with a tare of 4 t. 19 cwt. 2 qr. Ring bolts were spaced around wagon to secure sheets, and a sheet support fitted. Used for transport of sacks of grain, hay and other feeding stuffs, or any goods requiring cover in transit, and yet not wanting to be confined in a box wagon. Quite a considerable traffic in barrels of beer passed over the line — Oakhill Brewery, Binegar; Charlton and Anglo-Bavarian at Shepton Mallet; Hall & Woodhouse at Blandford and Holt Bros. at Burnham. Bricks and tiles from various brickyards were carried in this type of wagon. The lifting date of 19.7.04. dates this picture. Wagons were lifted by hydraulic jacks, wheels taken off and turned on lathe, underframe examined, nuts and bolts tightened. Wagon builders bored holes with a red hot poker to prevent the wood cracking. The Highbridge monogram 'HB' is on the solebar. Note the brake gear is on one side only but this was later duplicated.

Plate 71 is of a five-plank high-sided wagon No. 174, tare 4 t. 19 cwt. 0 qr. Although broadly similar to wagon No 141, there are differences: no sheet bar; lighter in weight; changed position of number plate and label holder; date of building, August 1887, is larger; separate builder's plate is fixed near the brake trunnion. The wagon is generally also in the Midland Railway style of livery.

Plate 72 is also a five-plank high-sided wagon No. 210, tare 5 t. 5 cwt. 2 qr. This is another variation of this type of goods wagon. Here the ends have been extended upwards, the centre being two boards (approximately 14-15 in.) higher than the wagon sides. Across the centre of the wagon end to end, is a wooden sheet support held in place by pins at each end to allow removal and thus ease loading and unloading. The axle box has also a different pattern cover. The sheep in the background of the photograph are in Broad Wharf, Highbridge.

Plate 73 is of a low-side wagon No. 689, tare 4 t. 15 cwt. 2 qr.; taken on No. 7 road at Bath Loco Depot, before the Victoria Works of Messrs. Stothert & Pitt were built. This siding branched from a Traffic Dept. siding (nearest in the photo) and was known as the 'Boat Road'. This gave access to the S&D Loco depot and the riverside sidings serving the grain shed and wharves, where barges were loaded and unloaded. The wagon had no doors, but individually sprung buffers, grease axle boxes and only one wooden brake block (on the far side). The operating lever was fulcrumed on the wagon underframe and extended to behind the left end far side wheel. The loop on

Plate 73: Wagon No. 689.

Author's Collection

Plate 74: Cattle truck No. 9.

Author's Collection

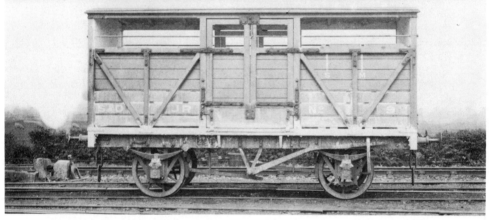

Plate 75: Cattle truck No. 1238.

Author's Collection

the left of the underframe was for use when being shunted by a horse.

The objects on the right of the picture are placed on the rails as safety stops, but later brakes were applied and sprags put through wheels when additional safety was required.

Plate 74 shows cattle truck No. 9, tare 6 t. 9 cwt. 5 qr. taken at the usual site by Highbridge Loco Works. There were a fair number of this type of truck in use and they usually ran as complete cattle trains to and from such markets as Sturminster Newton. Some single wagons were attached to the rear of passenger or perishable trains, while this type of wagon was in the majority when farm removal specials were needed.

The trucks were roughly padded inside to guard beasts from injury, while a padded partition was included with each vehicle and sometimes used. Although normally the truck was run 'large', i.e. without partition, the divider placed across the wagon at position 'M' made it medium size, while at 'S' it was small. The wide plank below the double doors dropped and formed a bridge to the floor of the cattle pen. Brakes were fitted one side only. The floor was periodically limewashed.

Plate 75 is of cattle truck No. 1238, tare 7 t. 6 cwt. 2 qr. This is a different type to No. 9, as instead of seven boards, it has only four side boards and the ventilation space has two rods across instead of one. Small metal plates indicate 'M' and 'S' position and the partition slides along the lower bar. The fall door consists of two planks. The lifting date is 30.4.04.

Axle boxes were oil lubricated and the covers were on a central pivot at the top and could be moved to and fro (at the bottom) for oil to be put into the reservoir base where it was siphoned up through worsted pads to the bearings. The label holder was rectangular instead of square. Again brake gear was fitted on only one side.

When the photographer painted out the background for publicity purposes he also removed one of the 3-link couplings.

Circa 1925, a cattle train ascending the bank out of Bath towards Devonshire Tunnel caught fire, a cinder probably igniting straw on the floor of a wagon. The bellowing of the cattle was painful to hear and a smell of roasting meat pervaded the area. A large pit was dug in the embankment near Beckhampton Road and the remains buried.

Plate 76 shows a ventilated meat van No. 1203, tare 7 t. 1 cwt. 1 qr. Inside the van were fastened insect-proof covers of zinc, perforated so finely that only air could pass through. Fitted to the van were burnished rods carrying burnished steel hooks on which sides of beef, mutton, pork etc., were hooked for transit. The fact that this van has chalked on it *All cheese come back* suggests that loading was not restricted only to meat. Note also the restriction: *To run between Highbridge and Nine Elms.* It had V-shaped spokes to the wheels and was fitted with oil lubrication axle boxes. Brakes were again only fitted to one side.

Plate 76: Van No. 1203.

Author's Collection

Plate 77: Road van No. 741.

Author's Collection

Plate 78: Van No. 1218.

Plate 79: Ballast Brake Van No. 1.

Plate 77 is of a ten-board road van No. 741, tare 5 t. 9 cwt. 1 qr. These road vans, or road boxes as they were often called, carried parcels, cheese, cattle cake, salt, flour, ironmongery, firebricks and other items which required protection from the weather. There was no large number plate, but a small, oval builder's plate fixed under the centre doors of the hinge type. Brake gear was only one side and the van had grease axle box lubrication. Although most of the background has been removed, the lower part of the 'Jim Crow' shows.

Plate 78 is of an eight-board slide door box wagon No. 1218. This van has a particularly plain appearance. Lifting date was 21.6.04; HB on left. On the right is small rectangular label holder which is blank, whereas usually they bear on top, the inscription *To Carry* and at the bottom the load in tons. The spring clip holds a *Not to Go* label and only the person who fitted the label had the authority to remove it, no matter what the circumstances. The roofs of Nos. 1203 and 1218 are quite plain being just covered with canvas glued to boards and painted, whereas usually a guide was provided to direct rain to the ends as on No. 741. No. 1218 had oil lubrication to the wheel bearings.

Plate 79 shows the ballast brake van No. 1 of the SDJR Engineer's Dept., tare 10 t. 2 cwt. 0 qr. This was a one-off job, built in 1904 and photographed at Highbridge in 1904. This was possibly the least-used van, but certainly the cleanest brake van on the S&D. It was kept at the Engineer's Dept headquarters at Glastonbury; painted red with black ironwork and white lettering. It was fitted out to carry workmen, and the running board and handrail saved men, when ballasting, many miles of walking along the rough track. It was open at the rear, where the brake wheel stood, with windows all round and the centre front opening so that the lamp-irons could be reached.

Wagon Miles over the Somerset & Dorset

During an average day in 1949 approximately 30,000 wagon miles were run over the S&D. On the day selected — a Thursday — 30,044 miles was the exact figure. Each individual goods guard's report was miled out by SFR and checked as to total miles of trains worked, with the engine miles as noted by the goods train drivers. The goods guards reports were then miled between each break of the load into the four sub classes:

Coal, coke, etc.	Other minerals	Goods & Livestock	Empty wagons	Engine & van
6,930 miles	2,683 miles	9,766 miles	10,665 miles	14 miles

Note: Only 81 miles of the 10,665 run by empty wagons were run in the 'down' direction

Chapter Ten

Other Activities

Plate 80: Writhlington Colliery.

British Rail

The S&DJR served a minor coalfield, important in its day. *Plate 80* is typical of this side of the railway activities and shows Writhlington Colliery, Radstock, c. 1900.

The photograph shows locomotive No. 25A with P.O. wagons that all appear to be fitted with dumb buffers and also note the signalbox has not yet been re-named 'BRAYSDOWN & WRITHLINGTON'.

The railway tracks remained unaltered until fairly recent years, except that the lines behind the signal box were taken away eliminating the triangle. The oval disc on the signal box indicates that all the electrical apparatus was working properly. If hung vertically it indicated to the telegraph lineman that there was a minor electrical fault, while if reversed showing a completely white face, immediate attention was needed. The three linemen were stationed at Highbridge, Blandford and Bath and between them travelled the

Plate 81: Steam crane at Bridgwater.

Author's Collection

Plate 82: Hydraulic crane at Highbridge.

Author's Collection

Plate 83: Steam crane at Highbridge.

line daily. The Highbridge lineman covered all the branch instruments; the Bath lineman, Bath to Evercreech Junction station, while the Blandford man covered Wimborne and Broadstone Junction to Evercreech Junction, the latter exclusive.

The Somerset & Dorset, for its size, was remarkably active in the marine field, and for a time ran a passenger steamer service from Burnham in Somerset to Cardiff. Its ketches and cargo steamers operated from Highbridge and Bridgwater, and these photographs give some insight into this side of the railway's activities.

Plate 81 is of the River Parrett Wharf, Bridgwater and shows a travelling steam crane, built by Thomas Smith, Leeds. There was never a cover for the driver and the running rails appear to be fastened to a concrete base or longitudinal sleepers. When the wharf closed in about 1920, the crane travelled to Highbridge under its own steam.

Plate 82 shows the Highbridge Wharf steam hydraulic crane No. 2 photographed in the 1890s. These cranes capable of lifting 1½ tons, were maintained in the best S&D tradition — treated as valuable property and although uncovered, all parts were cleaned and polished. Bill Spratt, driver of this one, earned 21s. for a 60-hour week. The crane ran on broad gauge track and the ship with a man at the masthead was the *Eliza*, of Gloucester.

Plate 83 also at Highbridge Wharf shows the winch steam crane, probably photographed pre-1900. The bowler-hatted man on the crane is Sidney Hall, the working steam crane foreman fitter. He was paid at the rate of 5s. 10d. per day (in 1897 increased to 6s. 8d. per day) and was always 'on call'. The land on the right is 'The Clyce', and further to the right is the new channel of the River Brue, with lock gates to control the outflow of fresh water and to prevent salt water pollution of the moors. On the left is a train of dead buffer single-bolster wagons loaded with rail and almost reaching the old weighbridge house. The ship by the crane is the *Providence*. She sank in the Bristol Channel in the late 1900s, loaded with coal from South Wales. A member of the crew was employed in the boilershop at the Loco Works after this mishap, and for the remainder of his life was known as 'Providence' W . . . .

Plate 84 is of the *S.S. Alpha* at Highbridge Wharf, photographed around 1895. The view shows the *Alpha* before lengthening in 1904 to carry the longer rails which were coming into use. She appears to be empty and waiting to sail out on the incoming tide. The *Alpha* and *Julia* were re-plated, the boilers removed and repaired by the boilermakers and fitters of Highbridge Works. Boats would berth at a quay near the old timber crane while the boilers were put on the quayside and this caused extra labour to be taken on. For example, men were engaged in March 1884 and discharged 17th May, 1884, when they had finished repairs to the *Alpha*.

The wagons are *(left to right)* No. 647; No. 676 (*To work between Highbridge Wharf & Burnham* – the three crosses may indicate its limited use); No. 47A *Loco Coal Highbridge* has three extra wide planks; No. 739 is a long low-side tube or plate wagon; No. 173 and the next wagon are both 5-plank high-sided wagons. A steam crane with cabin is on the wharf, with an open crane between wagons Nos. 739 and 173. The S&D sail loft was situated under the water tank at Burnham. A foreman and three sheetmakers were engaged with ships' sails, wagon and other sheets until the closure in 1930.

Plate 85 S.S. Leopard (seen here) was a successor to the sailing ketch *Julia*. On the quay behind the hut are piles of logs, while the wagon sheets to the left are painted 'SDJR 1296' and 'SDJR 1292'. The wagon on the extreme right and just visible above the wharf is a North Staffordshire Railway wagon with the county knot between the initials and number. The bucket below the hook of the hydraulic crane suggests that coal was unloaded at this quay, though it could have been grain, sand, or stone.

Plate 86 is again of *S.S. Julia*, built 1903 and photographed at Highbridge Wharf, probably at her breaking up in 1934. A Great Western Railway steam crane has lifted the boiler out and placed it on the right hand wagon.

Plate 84: S.S. Alpha at Highbridge.

British Rail

Plate 85: S.S. Leopard at Highbridge.

Author's Collection

Plate 86: S.S. Julia at Highbridge.

Plate 87: S.S. Radstock (the right hand steamer) at Highbridge.

Plate 87 was taken at Highbridge Wharf, in the late 1920s. The second ship (bought in 1925) seen on the left is the *S.S. Radstock* possibly unloading coal. For several months of the year, she and her sister ship the *S.S. Julia*, brought rails for the Southern Railway from South Wales to Highbridge, whence they were conveyed by rail to Templecombe. S&D ships also carried rails to Fremington, near Barnstaple. Shipping had, by this time, fallen considerably since the days of fair-sized timber boats from Baltic ports, and ketches three-abreast unloading coal. Only three steam cranes seem to remain out of about six (two hydraulic and at least four others). *S.S. Radstock* was finally broken up at Llanelli in February 1958.

Appendix One

Picture Parade

Plate 88: An interesting footplate view of a SDJR locomotive.

British Rail

Plate 89: 0-6-0T No. 8 seen in different livery to *Plate 24.*

British Rail

Plate 90: 0-4-4T No. 10, oldest of the Johnson Bogie Tanks.

British Rail

Plate 91: 0-4-4T No. 30 equipped with tablet catcher. Note the fire irons on tank top.

British Rail

Plate 92: 2-4-0 No. 15A as rebuilt in 1880.

British Rail

Plate 93: Small 4-4-0 No. 68, as rebuilt in 1908.

British Rail

Plate 94: Large 4-4-0 No. 77, built 1908.

British Rail

Plate 95: Large 4-4-0 No. 77, with footsteps added by rear bogie wheel and larger tender.

British Rail

Plate 96: Small 4-4-0 No. 14.

British Rail

Plate 97: Small 4-4-0 No. 17 in photographic grey livery.

British Rail

Plate 98: 'Bulldog' 0-6-0 No. 66 in photographic grey livery.

British Rail

Plate 99: 'Scottie Goods' 0-6-0 No. 28.

British Rail

Plates 100 and 101: Two views of Highbridge Works Gas Plant, taken on completion of building.

British Rail

Plate 102: Six-wheeled passenger brake van.

British Rail

Plate 103: coach No. 30.

British Rail

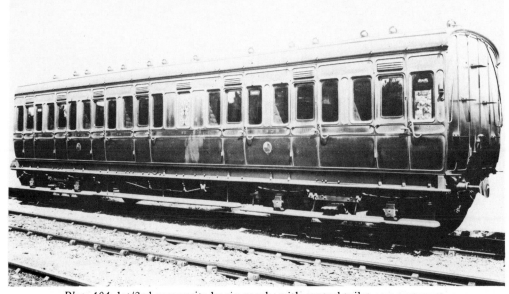

Plate 104: 1st/3rd composite bogie coach, with central toilet compartment.
British Rail

Plate 105: Third class bogie coach (note the safety coupling chains).
British Rail

Plate 106: Box van No. 1038.

British Rail

Plate 107: Horse box No. 1. The short wheelbase gave a rough ride when coupled to the rear of a passenger train. The groom rode in the compartment on the right.

British Rail

Plate 108: Gas tank wagon No. 2.

British Rail

Plate 109: Three-plank wagon No. 649.

British Rail

Plate 110: Hand crane and match truck.

British Rail

Timetables

DOWN BRANCH LINE

Distances	DOWN BRANCH LINE		Line	1B Passenger	2B Passenger and Milk Tanks to Templecombe	3B Passenger	4B Passenger	5B Passenger	6B Perishable & Tarif Vans	7B Passenger	8B Passenger	9B	10B Milk etc to Templecombe
M. C.				a.m.	a.m.	a.m.	p.m.	p.m.	p.m.	p.m.	p.m.	p.m.	p.m.
0 0	Burnham-on-Sea	dep.	1	9 45	..	11 20	2 10	3 0	..	6 25	7 5	..	..
1 50	Highbridge	arr.	2	9 50	z	11 25	2 15	3 5	..	6 30	7 10	..	..
		dep.	3	10 0	10 15			3 15	3 33	6 50			2 30
3 21	Bason Bridge	arr.	4	10 4	10 20	..	...	3 19	3 38	6 54			2 35
		dep.	5	10 5	10 25			3 25	4 38	6 57	...		3 0
6 60	Edington Junction	arr.	6	10 11	10 32	..		3 31	4 45	7 3			
13 75	Bridgwater	dep.	7	9 45	..		1 5	3 5	..	6 30			Sundays only
10 74	Bawdrip Halt	,,	8	9 52	..		1 12	3 12	..	6 37			
9 03	Cossington	,,	9	9 57	..		1 17	3 17	..	6 42			
6 60	Edington Junction	arr.	10	10 4	..		1 24	3 24	..	6 49			
8 74	Edington Junction	dep.	11	10 13	10 35			3 33	4 52	7 6			3 7
	Shapwick	arr.	12	10 18	10 40			3 39	4 58	7 11			
		dep.	13	10 19	10*45			3 41	5* 5	7 13			3 12
10 67	Ashcott	,,	14	10 24	10 51			3 46	5 19	7 17			
13 43	Glastonbury	arr.	15	10 30	10 58			3 52	5 27	7 24			
	Glastonbury	dep.	16	10A40			1 20	6 15	..	7 30			
16 51	Polsham Halt	,,	17	10 48			1 28	6 23	..	7 38			
18 76	Wells	arr.	18	10A56			1 34	6 29	..	7 44			
	Glastonbury	dep.	19	10 36	11 10			4 0	6 15	7 35			3 21
18 06	West Pennard	arr.	20	10 45	11 20			4 9	6 26	7 45			3 31
		dep.	21	10 46	11 23			4 12	7 0	7 48			3 50
22 17	Pylle	,,	22	10 54				4 20	..	7 56			
23 75	Evercreech Jct. North	pass	23	10 58	11 34			4 24	7 10	8 0			4 0
24 19	Evercreech Jct. Station	arr.	24	10Y59	11 35			4Y25	7 11	8Y 1			4 1

UP BRANCH LINE

Distances	UP BRANCH LINE		Line	1B Passenger	2B Passenger	3B Passenger	4B Passenger	5B Milk Tanks, etc, ex Templecombe	6B Passenger	7B Passenger	8B Passenger	9B	10B Milk, etc ex Templecombe
M. C.				a.m.	a.m.	p.m.	p.m.	p.m.	p.m.	p.m.	p.m.	p.m.	p.m.
0 0	Evercreech Jct. Station	dep.	1	..	10 0	12 45	..	4 30	..	5 45	9 25	..	6 5
0 24	Evercreech Jct. North	pass	2	..	10 1	12 46	..	..	..	5 46	9 26	..	6 6
2 2	Pylle	dep.	3	..	10 6	12 51	..	..	..	5 51	..	..	6 14
5 33	West Pennard	arr.	4	..	10 12	12 57	..	..	..	5 57	9 36	..	6 20
		dep.	5	..	10 14	12 59	..	4 41	..	5 58	9 38	..	6 26
10 56	Glastonbury	arr.	6	..	10 23	1 8	..	4 50	..	6 7	9 41	..	6 30
0 0	Wells	dep.	7	..	10A10	12 50	3 35	..	..	7A 0	..	..	..
2 30	Polsham Halt	,,	8	..	10 18	12 57	3 42	..	..	7 8	..	..	..
5 33	Glastonbury	arr.	9	..	10A26	1 3	3 48	..	..	7A16	..	..	..
	Glastonbury	dep.	10	8A15	10*33	1 15	..	4 52	..	6 13	9 48	..	6 52
13 32	Ashcott	,,	11	8 23	10 40	1 22	..	..	..	6 20	..	..	..
15 25	Shapwick	arr.	12	8 29	10 44	1 26	..	..	..	6 24	..	..	..
		dep.	13	8 30	10*46	1 27	..	5 1	..	6 25	9 58	..	7 1
17 39	Edington Junction	arr.	14	8A36	10 51	1 32	..	..	..	6 31	10 3	..	..
	Edington Junction	dep.	15	..	10 55	1 40	3A40	..	..	7 5	..	..	Sundays only
20 42	Cossington	,,	16	..	11 2	1 47	3 47	..	..	7 12	..	..	
21 53	Bawdrip Halt	,,	17	..	11 6	1 51	3 51	..	..	7 16	..	..	
24 54	Bridgwater	arr.	18	..	11 13	1 57	3A57	..	..	7 22	..	..	
	Edington Junction	dep.	19	..	10 53	1 35	..	5 6	..	6 33	10 5	..	7 6
20 78	Bason Bridge	arr.	20	..	10 59	1 41	..	5 12	..	6 39	..	..	7 13
		dep.	21	..	11 1	1 50	..	5 30	..	6 41	..	..	7 20
22 41	Highbridge Station	arr.	22	..	11 5	1 54	..	5 35	..	6 45	10Y15	..	7 25
		dep.	23	9 30	11 10	2 0	2 50	..	6 0	6 55	..	..	..
24 19	Burnham-on-Sea	arr.	24	9Y35	11Y15	2Y 5	2Y55	..	6Y 5	7Y 0	..	..	..

Somerset and Dorset Working Timetable of 1940 showing Passenger and Milk Trains.

Reporting Nos.		51B	52B	53B	54B	55B	56B	57B	58B	59B
DOWN BRANCH LINE.		Freight.	Freight.	Light Engine.	Freight.	Freight.	Freight to T'Combe.	Fitted Freight 1 to Bath.	Freight to T'Combe.	Freight to T'Combe.
Miles.		a.m.	a.m.	WO a.m.	p.m.	p.m.	p.m.	Q p.m. N P	Q p.m. N	p.m.
0 0	Burnham-on-Sea ¶ dep.	..	..	..	..	4 10	..	..	..	
1 17	Highbridge Wharf ¶ ,,	..	6 50	..	12 30	4A15	5 35	..	7 0	
1 50	Highbridge Stn... arr.	..	6063	..	..	..	5 38	..	..	From Bridgwater.
	⚒ dep.	5 30	6 65	10 15	12*53	..	5G50	5 48	7 5	
3 21	Bason Bridge.... arr.	5 36	..	..	12 38	A—Arrival time	5 55	5 52	7 8	
	dep.	6 25	..	..	..		6 8	6 15	7 20	
6 60	Edington Jc. .... arr.	6 35	..	10 23	..		6 18	6 23	7 30	10 8
	⚒ dep.	..	7 10	10 25	..		6 25	6 30	7 35	10 25
8 74	Shapwick ...... arr.	..	7 17	..	..		6B32	..	7B42	..
	⚒ dep.	..	7 33	..	..		6 42	6 35	7 45	10 32
.. ..	Alexander's Siding arr.	..	7 37	..	..		..	..	..	..
	dep.	..	7 48	..	..	To Bridgwater.	..	..	..	B
10 67	Ashcott .... arr.	..	7 52	..	..		..	..	..	
	dep.	..	8 3	..	..		..	..	..	
13 43	Glastonbury .... arr.	..	8 11	..	..		6 55	6 45	8 0	10 47
	⚒ dep.	..	10 50	..	..		8 35	6 55	8D45	11 5
18 66	West Pennard .. arr.	..	11D 4	..	..		8 49	..	8 59	..
	⚒ dep.	..	11 50	..	..		9 0	7 6	9 45	11B19
22 17	Pylle .... arr.	..	..	..	..		..	..	..	
	dep.	..	..	..	..		..	..	..	
23 75	Evercreech Jc. N. ⚒ arr.	..	12 10	..	..		9 20	7 17	10 5	11F39
	dep.	..	..	..	..		..	7 33	10 30	1½0

Reporting Nos.		51B	52B	53B	54B	55B	56B	57B	58B
UP BRANCH LINE.		Freight from T'Combe.	Freight.	Freight.	Freight.	Freight.	Light Engine.	Freight from T'Combe.	
Miles.		a.m.	p.m.	a.m.	p.m.	p.m.	p.m.	WO p.m.	
0 24	Evercreech Jc.Nth. arr.	5 12	..	..	..	..	..	6 12	
	⚒ dep.	6 15	..	11 5	..	..	..	7 45	
2 2	Pylle .... arr.	..	..	11 11	..	..	From Bridgwater.	..	
	dep.	..	..	11 20	..	..		..	
5 33	West Pennard .. arr.	..	..	11 30	..	..		..	
	⚒ dep.	6 31	..	12D25	..	..		8 1	
10 56	Glastonbury .... arr.	6 45	..	12 39	..	..		8 15	
	⚒ dep.	8 15	..	1 25	..	..		9D20	
13 32	Ashcott .... arr.	..	..	..	..	..		..	
	dep.	..	..	..	..	..	A—Departure time	..	
15 25	Shapwick ...... arr.	8 26	..	1 36	..	..		..	
	⚒ dep.	8*35	..	1 55	..	..		9 31	
17 39	Edington Jc. .... arr.	8 41	..	2 1	..	..	5 10	9 37	
	⚒ dep.	8 50	..	2 25	12 0	..	5 12	9 42	
20 78	Bason Bridge.... arr.	..	..	..	..	..		..	
	dep.	..	1 10	..	..	..		..	
22 41	Highbridge Stn...⚒ arr.	To Bridgwater.	..	..	..	..	5 20	..	
	dep.		1 16	2 40	12 13	..	..	9 57	
23 02	Highbridge Wharf ¶ arr.		1 19	2 43	12 16	..	3A10	10 0	
24 19	Burnham-on-Sea ¶ arr.		..	..	..	..	3 15	..	

B—Stops for Road Van Traffic only if necessary.
D—Change Trainmen.
G—Worked by G.W. Engine.
N—Loaded Traffic only must be forwarded by this train.
P—When this train runs, the 5.35 p.m. Highbridge Wharf to Evercreech Junction will be cancelled and the 7.0 p.m. from Highbridge Wharf will run in lieu thereof.

Freight-Working Timetable for 1938.